This journal belongs to

_____

When peace, like a river, attendeth my way,
When sorrows like sea billows roll;
Whatever my lot, Thou hast taught me to say,
It is well, it is well, with my soul.

HORATIO G. SPAFFORD

The LORD is my shepherd; I shall not want. He makes me to lie down in green pastures; He leads me beside the still waters. He restores my soul.

PSALM 23:1-3 NKJV

Jesus stood and said...“Let anyone who is thirsty come to me and drink. Whoever believes in me, as Scripture has said, rivers of living water will flow from within them.”

JOHN 7:37–38 NIV

We must drink deeply from the very Source the deep calm and peace of
interior quietude and refreshment of God, allowing the pure water
of divine grace to flow plentifully and unceasingly from the Source itself.

MOTHER TERESA

Come and sit and ask Him whatever is on your heart. No question is
too small, no riddle too simple. He has all the time in the world.
Come and seek the will of God.

MAX LUCADO

Trust in the LORD with all your heart; do not depend on your own understanding.
Seek his will in all you do, and he will show you which path to take.

PROVERBS 3:5–6 NLT

The signposts of GOD are clear and point out the right road.
The life-maps of GOD are right, showing the way to joy.

PSALM 19:7-8 MSG

_____

_____

_____

_____

_____

_____

_____

_____

_____

_____

_____

_____

_____

_____

_____

_____

_____

_____

_____

_____

We are not alone on our journey. The God of love who gave us life sent us
[His] only Son to be with us at all times and in all places, so that we never
have to feel lost in our struggles but always can trust that God walks with us.

HENRI J. M. NOUWEN

Stillness is a state of calm. Nothing brings calm like prayer, nor will anything restore your peace like the quietness of conversation with God. Stillness is a form of waiting. And stillness is faith in the peace that is coming.

_Since we have been justified through faith, we have peace with God
through our Lord Jesus Christ, through whom we have gained
access by faith into this grace in which we now stand._

ROMANS 5:1–2 NIV

*I know the L*ORD *is always with me. I will not be shaken, for he is right beside me. No wonder my heart is glad, and I rejoice. My body rests in safety.*

PSALM 16:8–9 NLT

_____

_____

_____

_____

_____

_____

_____

_____

_____

_____

_____

_____

_____

_____

_____

_____

_____

This is peace—to be able to sleep in the storm! In Christ, we are relaxed
and at peace in the midst of the confusions...and perplexities of
this life. The storm rages, but our hearts are at rest.

BILLY GRAHAM

When we lay the soil of our hard lives open to the rain of grace and let joy penetrate our cracked and dry places, let joy soak into our broken skin and deep crevices, *life* grows. How can this not be the best thing for the world?... The clouds open when we mouth thanks.

ANN VOSKAMP

See, I am doing a new thing! Now it springs up; do you not perceive it?
I am making a way in the wilderness and streams in the wasteland.

ISAIAH 43:19 NIV

Who are those who fear the LORD? He will show them the path they should choose.

PSALM 25:12 NLT

_____

_____

_____

_____

_____

_____

_____

_____

_____

_____

_____

_____

_____

_____

_____

_____

_____

_____

_____

However things may appear to be, of all possible circumstances—those circumstances in whose midst I am set—these are the best that He could choose for me. We do not know how this is true—where would faith be if we did?—but we do know that all things that happen are full of shining seed.

The peace of God is that eternal calm which lies far too deep down
to be reached by any external trouble or disturbance.

ARTHUR T. PIERSON

_____

_____

_____

_____

_____

_____

_____

_____

_____

_____

_____

_____

_____

_____

In waiting we begin to get in touch with the rhythms of life
stillness and action, listening and decision. They are the
rhythms of God. It is in the everyday and the commonplace
that we learn patience, acceptance, and contentment.

RICHARD J. FOSTER

There is a peace here, a serenity, even before I enter. Just the idea of returning becomes a balm for the wounds I've collected elsewhere. Before I can finish even one knock, the door opens wide and I am in His presence.

BARBARA FARMER

Keep on asking.... Keep on seeking.... Keep on knocking.... For everyone who asks, receives.
Everyone who seeks, finds. And to everyone who knocks, the door will be opened.

He gives strength to the weary and increases the power of the weak. Even youths grow tired and weary...but those who hope in the LORD will renew their strength.

ISAIAH 40:29–31 NIV

_____

_____

_____

_____

_____

_____

_____

_____

_____

_____

_____

_____

_____

_____

_____

_____

Your heavenly Father is reaching for your hand. He knows you
work hard. He knows you give your all but sometimes come up short.
He knows when you're worn out by life and feel faint in your faith.
God wants you to simply put your hand in His—and trust.
He promises to exchange His strength for your weariness.

I will let God's peace infuse every part of today. As the chaos swirls and life's demands pull at me on all sides, I will breathe in God's peace that surpasses all understanding. He has promised that He would set within me a peace too deeply planted to be affected by unexpected or exhausting demands.

_____

_____

_____

_____

_____

_____

_____

_____

_____

_____

_____

_____

_____

Blessed are those who trust in the LORD.... They are like trees planted along a riverbank, with roots that reach deep into the water.

JEREMIAH 17:7-8 NLT

Give your entire attention to what God is doing right now, and don't
get worked up about what may or may not happen tomorrow.
God will help you deal with whatever...when the time comes.

MATTHEW 6:34 MSG

Thank the Lord, it is His love that arranges our tomorrows—and we may be
certain that whatever tomorrow brings, His love sent it our way.

CHARLES SWINDOLL

We have a Father in heaven who is almighty, who loves His children as He loves His only-begotten Son, and whose very joy and delight it is to... help them at all times and under all circumstances.

GEORGE MUELLER

_____

_____

_____

_____

_____

_____

_____

_____

_____

_____

_____

_____

_____

_____

_____

_____

Let us draw near with confidence to the throne of grace,
so that we may receive mercy and find grace to help in time of need.

HEBREWS 4:16 NASB

When my anxious thoughts multiply within me, Your consolations delight my soul.

PSALM 94:19 NASB

God comforts. He doesn't pity. He picks us up, dries our tears,
soothes our fears, and lifts our thoughts beyond the hurt.

Dr. Robert Schuller

I think we like to be constantly doing because it validates our existence....
But, God says to be content. He calls us—not to be lazy and never get
anything done—but to balance our work with rest. And even when we're
at work to rest our souls in Him. Not to be always thinking, analyzing,
and planning, but to stay our minds on Him and live in peace.

GWEN FORD FAULKENBERRY

You will keep him in perfect peace, whose mind is stayed on You, because he trusts in You.

ISAIAH 26:3 NKJV

The peace of God, which transcends all understanding,
will guard your hearts and your minds in Christ Jesus.

PHILIPPIANS 4:7 NIV

_____

_____

_____

_____

_____

_____

_____

_____

_____

_____

_____

_____

_____

_____

_____

_____

All [God's] glory and beauty come from within, and there He
delights to dwell. His visits there are frequent, His conversation sweet,
His comforts refreshing, His peace passing all understanding.

THOMAS À KEMPIS

Authentic hope is the confidence that no matter what the outcome, God will see you through all of life's challenges and difficulties. That's not wishful thinking; that's a certainty. That requires a shift from insisting upon a particular way you think things should go to deciding that no matter how things go, God will be your constant companion and source of comfort.

Hope does not disappoint, because the love of God has been poured out
within our hearts through the Holy Spirit who was given to us.

ROMANS 5:5 NASB

Are you tired? Worn out? Burned out on religion? Come to me. Get away with me and you'll recover your life. I'll show you how to take a real rest. Walk with me and work with me—watch how I do it. Learn the unforced rhythms of grace.

MATTHEW 11:28-29 MSG

The fruit of our placing all things in His hands
is the presence of His abiding peace in our hearts.

HANNAH WHITALL SMITH

Christ desires to be with you in whatever crisis you may find yourself. Call upon His name. See if He will not do as He promised He would. He will not make your problems go away, but He will give you the power to deal with and overcome them.

BILLY GRAHAM

I can do all this through him who gives me strength.

For the Kingdom of God is not a matter of what we eat or drink,
but of living a life of goodness and peace and joy in the Holy Spirit.

ROMANS 14:17 NLT

_____

_____

_____

_____

_____

_____

_____

_____

_____

_____

_____

_____

_____

_____

Joy is not happiness so much as gladness; it is the ecstasy of eternity
in a soul that has made peace with God and is ready to do His will.

The Bible is full of stories of people whose backs were up against the wall.... Often they had nothing—no food to feed their families, no cure for their diseases, no money to pay their taxes, no hope that life could ever again be right. In their darkest moments, they discovered a God whose love and power went far beyond their wildest expectations.

God can do anything, you know—far more than you could ever imagine
or guess or request in your wildest dreams! He does it...by working
within us, his Spirit deeply and gently within us.

Ephesians 3:20–21 MSG

Though I have fallen, I will rise. Though I sit in darkness, the LORD will be my light.

MICAH 7:8 NIV

We always hope that God will lift us *above* our circumstances.
And sometimes He does. But much of the time He walks us *through*
them so we can learn a new dimension of His power.

Stormie Omartian

In comparison with this big world, the human heart is only a small thing. Though the world is so large, it is utterly unable to satisfy this tiny heart. Our ever-growing soul and its capacities can be satisfied only in the infinite God. As water is restless until it reaches its level, so the soul has no peace until it rests in God.

SADHU SUNDAR SINGH

Satisfy us in the morning with your unfailing love,
that we may sing for joy and be glad all our days.

We take our lead from Christ, who is the source of everything we do.

EPHESIANS 4:16 MSG

_____

_____

_____

_____

_____

_____

_____

_____

_____

_____

_____

_____

_____

_____

_____

_____

_____

_____

He is the Source. Of everything. Strength for your day. Wisdom
for your task. Comfort for your soul. Grace for your battle.
Provision for each need. Understanding for each failure.
Assistance for every encounter.

JACK HAYFORD

When you recognize every good gift ultimately comes from God, you can't help but feel grateful. This deepens the pleasure of even an ordinary day, making you not only more content, but more generous with what you've received.

Every good and perfect gift is from above, coming down from the Father
of the heavenly lights, who does not change like shifting shadows.

JAMES 1:17 NIV

If GOD hadn't been there for me, I never would have made it. The minute I said, "I'm slipping, I'm falling," your love, God, took hold and held me fast.

PSALM 94:17–18 MSG

How much greater is my peace when I find it has come
in the midst of the storm and not because He stilled its forces.

LEITA TWYEFFORT

Our inner happiness depends not on what we experience but on the degree of our gratitude to God, whatever the experience.

ALBERT SCHWEITZER

Rejoice always, pray continually, give thanks in all circumstances;
for this is God's will for you in Christ Jesus.

1 THESSALONIANS 5:16-18 NIV

Though the mountains be shaken and the hills be removed,
yet my unfailing love for you will not be shaken.

ISAIAH 54:10 NIV

_____

_____

_____

_____

_____

_____

_____

_____

_____

_____

_____

_____

_____

_____

_____

Count on God's personal love for you. He won't leave, won't walk out, won't betray. He isn't a human capable of erratic tendencies. His promise to stand by you is bankable. So when life circumstances are unsettled, you can have perfect peace because the one who steadily sustains you doesn't shift, slip, warp, crack, disappear, or change.

If peace be in the heart, the wildest winter storm is full of solemn beauty....
Each living creature tells some new and joyous story,
The very trees and stones all catch a ray of glory,
If peace be in the heart.

C. F. RICHARDSON

The LORD your God in your midst, The Mighty One, will save;
He will rejoice over you with gladness, He will quiet you with His love,
He will rejoice over you with singing.

ZEPHANIAH 3:17 NKJV

We know that in all things God works for the good of those who love him,
who have been called according to his purpose.

ROMANS 8:28 NIV

Dear God...I surrender to You the situations I face that I feel
I cannot accept. Although I get impatient for these things to change,
help me to learn to be content and peaceful in the midst of them because...
I trust that You love me enough to always bring good out of the situation.

STORMIE OMARTIAN

Where the soul is full of peace and joy, outward surroundings
and circumstances are of comparatively little account.

HANNAH WHITALL SMITH

Behold, God is my helper; the Lord is the sustainer of my soul.
Psalm 54:4 nasb

He who watches over you will not slumber.... The sun will not harm you by day, nor the moon by night.... The LORD will watch over your coming and going both now and forevermore.

PSALM 121:3, 6, 8 NIV

_____

_____

_____

_____

_____

_____

_____

_____

_____

_____

_____

_____

_____

_____

_____

_____

Have courage for the great sorrows of life, and patience
for the small ones; and when you have…accomplished
your daily task, go to sleep in peace. God is awake.

VICTOR HUGO

There will be times in life when nothing makes any sense. We hoped for something great and came up empty. But be assured that even in this place of darkness, God is present. Throughout history, every great work of God started in this exact place of emptiness. God fills those things that are empty.

_You don't need a telescope, a microscope, or a horoscope to realize the
fullness of Christ, and the emptiness of the universe without him.
When you come to him, that fullness comes together for you, too._

COLOSSIANS 2:7–9 MSG

The LORD is trustworthy in all he promises and faithful in all he does.

PSALM 145:13 NIV

God is the God of promise. He keeps His word, even when that seems
impossible; even when the circumstances seem to point to the opposite.

COLIN URQUHART

Dear Father, my days are so full and I find myself overwhelmed.
Give me the peace that comes from knowing that where I am,
You are, and together we can handle whatever comes.

PAM KIDD

Hear my cry, O God; attend to my prayer. From the end of the earth I will cry to You,
when my heart is overwhelmed; lead me to the rock that is higher than I.
For You have been a shelter for me.

PSALM 61:1–3 NKJV

"LORD, help!" they cried in their trouble, and he saved them from their distress.
He calmed the storm to a whisper and stilled the waves.
What a blessing was that stillness as he brought them safely into harbor!

PSALM 107:28–30 NLT

_____

_____

_____

_____

_____

_____

_____

_____

_____

_____

_____

_____

_____

Only Christ Himself, who slept in the boat in the storm and then spoke calm
to the wind and waves, can stand beside us when we are in a panic and say
to us Peace. It will not be explainable. It transcends human understanding.
And there is nothing else like it in the whole wide world.

ELISABETH ELLIOT

True contentment is a real, even an active, virtue—not only affirmative but creative. It is the power of getting out of any situation all there is in it.

G. K. CHESTERTON

Do you want to stand out? Then step down. Be a servant.
If you puff yourself up, you'll get the wind knocked out of you. But if
you're content to simply be yourself, your life will count for plenty.

MATTHEW 23:11–12 MSG

By awesome deeds You answer us in righteousness, O God of our salvation,
You who are the trust of all the ends of the earth and of the farthest sea....
Who stills the roaring of the seas, the roaring of their waves,
And the tumult of the peoples.

PSALM 65:5, 7 NASB

_____

_____

_____

_____

_____

_____

_____

_____

_____

_____

_____

_____

_____

_____

_____

_____

_____

_____

The crashing wave finally reaches peace as it breaks upon the land…so our
turbulent spirits find rest as we break upon the vast shoreline of God's love.

JANET L. SMITH

We cannot believe that a writer is a terrible person simply because the hero of the book goes through terrible times. On the contrary, we believe that a good author won't leave the hero in despair. A good author will provide a way out.

In the same way, when we come to God with our burdens, we must understand that the story isn't over. God is ready to write the best possible ending to each person's life.

No test or temptation that comes your way is beyond the course of what others have had to face. All you need to remember is that God will never let you down...he'll always be there to help you come through it.

1 CORINTHIANS 10:13 MSG

The Son is the image of the invisible God, the firstborn over all creation. For in him all things were created.... He is before all things, and in him all things hold together.

COLOSSIANS 1:15-17 NIV

God may be invisible, but He's in touch. You may not be able to see Him, but He is in control. And that includes you—your circumstances. That includes what you've just lost. That includes what you've just gained. That includes all of life—past, present, future.

CHARLES SWINDOLL

God's holy beauty comes near you, like a spiritual scent, and it stirs your drowsing soul…. He creates in you the desire to find Him and run after Him—to follow wherever He leads you, and to press peacefully against His heart wherever He is.

JOHN OF THE CROSS

You will call on me and come and pray to me, and I will listen to you.
You will seek me and find me when you seek me with all your heart.

God's Spirit touches our spirits and confirms who we really are.
We know who he is, and we know who we are: Father and children.

ROMANS 8:15–16 MSG

_____

_____

_____

_____

_____

_____

_____

_____

_____

_____

_____

_____

_____

_____

_____

_____

_____

I know that [the Lord] loves me, even though I do not feel that love
as I can feel a human embrace, even though I do not hear a voice
as I hear human words of consolation.... God is greater than my
senses, greater than my thoughts, greater than my heart. I do believe
that He touches me in places that are unknown even to myself.

HENRI J. M. NOUWEN

Finding acceptance with joy, whatever the circumstances of life—whether they are petty annoyances or fiery trials—this is a living faith that grows.

MARY LOU STEIGLEDER

I know what it is to be in need, and I know what it is to have plenty.
I have learned the secret of being content in any and every situation.

We've been surrounded and battered by troubles, but we're not demoralized;
we're not sure what to do, but we know that God knows what to do;...
we've been thrown down, but we haven't broken. What they did to Jesus,
they do to us...; what Jesus did among them, he does in us—he lives!

2 CORINTHIANS 4:8–10 MSG

_____

_____

_____

_____

_____

_____

_____

_____

_____

_____

_____

_____

_____

_____

_____

_____

When disappointment leaves you discouraged, remember God has
something better in mind. Trade your heartache for anticipation
as you wait for the beauty of God's plan to unfold.

Calm me, O Lord, as You stilled the storm,
Still me, O Lord, keep me from harm.
Let all the tumult within me cease,
Enfold me, Lord, in Your peace.

CELTIC TRADITIONAL

I am leaving you with a gift—peace of mind and heart. And the peace I give
is a gift the world cannot give. So don't be troubled or afraid.

JOHN 14:27 NLT

The joy of the LORD is your strength.

NEHEMIAH 8:10 NKJV

_____

_____

_____

_____

_____

_____

_____

_____

_____

_____

_____

_____

_____

_____

_____

_____

Joy cannot be pursued. It comes from within. It is a state of being.
It does not depend on circumstances, but triumphs over circumstances.
It produces a gentleness of spirit and a magnetic personality.

BILLY GRAHAM

Gratitude unlocks the fullness of life. It turns what we have into enough, and more. It turns denial into acceptance, chaos to order, confusion to clarity. It can turn a meal into a feast, a house into a home, a stranger into a friend. Gratitude makes sense of our past, brings peace for today, and creates a vision for tomorrow.

MELODY BEATTIE

Whatever you do, whether in word or deed, do it all in the name of the Lord Jesus,
giving thanks to God the Father through him.

COLOSSIANS 3:17 NIV

Now faith is confidence in what we hope for and assurance about what we do not see.

HEBREWS 11:1 NIV

———————————————————————

———————————————————————

———————————————————————

———————————————————————

———————————————————————

———————————————————————

———————————————————————

———————————————————————

———————————————————————

———————————————————————

———————————————————————

———————————————————————

———————————————————————

Those who know God have great contentment in God. There is no peace like the peace of those whose minds are possessed with full assurance that they have known God, and God has known them, and that this relationship guarantees God's favor to them in life, through death, and on forever.

J. I. PACKER

Only God gives true peace—a quiet gift He sets within us
just when we think we've exhausted our search for it.

Now may the God of peace make you holy in every way, and may your whole spirit and soul and body be kept blameless until our Lord Jesus Christ comes again. God will make this happen, for he who calls you is faithful.

1 THESSALONIANS 5:23–24 NLT

I pray that your love will overflow more and more, and that you will keep on growing in knowledge and understanding. For I want you to understand what really matters, so that you may live pure and blameless lives until the day of Christ's return.

PHILIPPIANS 1:9–10 NLT

_____

_____

_____

_____

_____

_____

_____

_____

_____

_____

_____

_____

_____

_____

_____

_____

_____

As God helps you see more clearly what really matters in this world, contentment spreads its sense of peaceful appreciation deeper into your soul. That hunger to strive for more is replaced by a hunger to know more of God. That's what lies at the heart of living a full life.

Life from the Center is a life of unhurried peace and power. It is simple. It is serene.... We need not get frantic. He is at the helm. And when our little day is done, we lie down quietly in peace, for all is well.

THOMAS R. KELLY

I will both lie down in peace, and sleep; for You alone, O LORD, make me dwell in safety.

PSALM 4:8 NKJV

The LORD is my strength and my shield; my heart trusts in him, and he helps me. My heart leaps for joy, and with my song I praise him.

PSALM 28:7 NIV

_____

_____

_____

_____

_____

_____

_____

_____

_____

_____

_____

_____

_____

_____

_____

_____

_____

Heavenly Father, my prayer is that I would learn to trust You more. It's such
a comfort to know that my life is in Your hands, and the circumstances
surrounding me are in Your control. Remind me daily that choosing to be
happy is an option. May I find my strength in Your joy. Amen.

KIM BOYCE

No one can get inner peace by pouncing on it, by vigorously willing to have it. Peace is a margin of power around our daily need. Peace is a consciousness of springs too deep for earthly droughts to dry up.

HARRY EMERSON FOSDICK

_____

_____

_____

_____

_____

_____

_____

_____

_____

_____

_____

_____

_____

_____

_____

_____

_____

_____

_____

The LORD will guide you always; he will satisfy your needs in a sun-scorched land and will strengthen your frame. You will be like a well-watered garden, like a spring whose waters never fail.

ISAIAH 58:11 NIV

Be of good courage, and He shall strengthen your heart, all you who hope in the LORD.
PSALM 31:24 NKJV

_____

_____

_____

_____

_____

_____

_____

_____

_____

_____

_____

_____

_____

_____

_____

Should we feel at times disheartened and discouraged, a simple movement
of heart toward God will renew our powers. Whatever He may demand of us,
He will give us at the moment the strength and courage that we need.

FRANÇOIS FÉNELON

Peace is an awareness of reserves from beyond ourselves,
so that our power is not so much in us as through us.

I pray that God, the source of hope, will fill you completely with joy and peace because you trust in him. Then you will overflow with confident hope through the power of the Holy Spirit.

ROMANS 15:13 NLT

Godliness with contentment is great gain. For we brought nothing into the world, and we can take nothing out of it. But if we have food and clothing, we will be content with that.

I TIMOTHY 6:6-8 NIV

Becoming content with your life isn't an impossible goal to strive for; it's a reality that's available to you now. Gratitude for what God has already given you is an essential element in learning to be content. Thank God for His provision, and rest in the knowledge that He will continue to provide.

The miracle of joy is this: It happens when there is no apparent reason for it. Circumstances may call for despair. Yet something different rouses itself inside us.... We are able to remember what the sunrise looks like.... We remember God. We remember He is love. We remember He is near.

RUTH SENTER

Look to the LORD and his strength; seek his face always.
Remember the wonders he has done.

PSALM 105:4-5 NIV

See what great love the Father has lavished on us, that we should be called children of God! And that is what we are!

1 JOHN 3:1 NIV

_____

_____

_____

_____

_____

_____

_____

_____

_____

_____

_____

_____

_____

_____

_____

_____

_____

May God kiss you with His peace, as a father kisses his little child.
And may you know that peace isn't a pot of gold rewarded to you
after chasing some rainbow's end—it's a gift.

Hear me say YES! Not "I'm worried." Not "I'm stressed out."... Hear me say *thank you*.... Watch me *live a life* of yes. To all that was and is and is to come.... The God whom we thank for fulfilling the promises of the past will fulfill His promises again. In Christ, the answer to the questions of every moment is always Yes.

ANN VOSKAMP

For all of God's promises have been fulfilled in Christ with a resounding "Yes!"
And through Christ, our "Amen" (which means "Yes") ascends to God for his glory.

2 CORINTHIANS 1:20 NLT

Now may the Lord of peace himself give you his peace at all times and in every situation. The Lord be with you all.

2 THESSALONIANS 3:16 NLT

_____

_____

_____

_____

_____

_____

_____

_____

_____

_____

_____

_____

_____

_____

_____

_____

_____

_____

_____

_____

_____

_____

_____

_____

_____

_____

_____

_____

_____

_____

_____

_____

_____

Live for today but hold your hands open to tomorrow. Anticipate the future and its changes with joy. There is a seed of God's love in every event, every circumstance, every…situation in which you may find yourself.

BARBARA JOHNSON

Love comes while we rest against our Father's chest.

Joy comes when we catch the rhythms of His heart.

Peace comes when we live in harmony with those rhythms.

KEN GIRE

I want you woven into a tapestry of love, in touch with everything there is to know of God. Then you will have minds confident and at rest, focused on Christ.

COLOSSIANS 2:2 MSG

So do not worry, saying, "What shall we eat?" or "What shall we drink?"
or "What shall we wear?"… But seek first his kingdom and his righteousness,
and all these things will be given to you as well.

MATTHEW 6:31, 33 NIV

_____

_____

_____

_____

_____

_____

_____

_____

_____

_____

_____

_____

_____

_____

_____

_____

Today I give it all to Jesus...my hopes, my plans and
dreams and schemes, my fears and failures—all.
Peace and contentment come when the struggle ceases.

GLORIA GAITHER

The God who created the vast resources of the universe is also the
inventor of the human mind. His inspired words of encouragement
guarantee us that we can live above our circumstances.

DR. JAMES DOBSON

Why do you say…"My way is hidden from the LORD;
my cause is disregarded by my God"? Do you not know? Have you not heard?
The LORD is the everlasting God, the Creator of the ends of the earth.

ISAIAH 40:27–28 NIV

You keep track of all my sorrows. You have collected all my tears in your bottle. You have recorded each one in your book.

PSALM 56:8 NLT

_____

_____

_____

_____

_____

_____

_____

_____

_____

_____

_____

_____

_____

_____

_____

_____

Only God can heal the sorrow you feel. His gifts of peace, comfort,
and compassion may feel elusive at times. But remember, feelings
don't paint an accurate picture of the truth. Keep reaching out
to Him, even when tears are all you have to offer.

I have held many things in my hands and I have lost them all;
but whatever I have placed in God's hands, that I still possess.

MARTIN LUTHER

Do not store up for yourselves treasures on earth, where moth and rust destroy, and where thieves break in and steal. But store up for yourselves treasures in heaven, where neither moth nor rust destroys, and where thieves do not break in or steal; for where your treasure is, there your heart will be also.

MATTHEW 6:19–21 NASB

*May God give you more and more grace and peace as you grow
in your knowledge of God and Jesus our Lord.*

2 PETER 1:2 NLT

He gives more grace when the burdens grow greater,
He sends more strength when the labors increase;
To added affliction he adds his mercy,
To multiplied trials, His multiplied peace.

ANNIE JOHNSON FLINT

Dear Lord.... When I read Your Word, peace and contentment fill my heart....
Help me to understand the truth that is in the Scriptures so that I will always
stand on the solid foundation it gives me. When I read of Your laws, I see that
they are good and reliable, and when I live by them, life works.

STORMIE OMARTIAN

Great peace have those who love Your law, and nothing causes them to stumble.

What happens when we live God's way? He brings gifts into our lives, much the same way that fruit appears in an orchard—things like affection for others, exuberance about life, serenity.

GALATIANS 5:22 MSG

_____

_____

_____

_____

_____

_____

_____

_____

_____

_____

_____

_____

_____

_____

Over the margins of life comes a whisper, a faint call, a premonition of richer living which we know we are passing by. Strained by the very mad pace of our daily outer burdens, we are further strained by an inward uneasiness, because we have hints that there is a way of life vastly richer and deeper than all this hurried existence, a life of unhurried serenity and peace and power.

THOMAS R. KELLY

Emptiness itself can birth the fullness of grace because in the emptiness
we have the opportunity to turn to God, the only begetter of Grace,
and there find all the fullness of joy, peace, rest.

ANN VOSKAMP

You will show me the way of life, granting me the joy of your presence and the pleasures of living with you forever.

The LORD is close to the brokenhearted and saves those who are crushed in spirit.
PSALM 34:18 NIV

_____

_____

_____

_____

_____

_____

_____

_____

_____

_____

_____

_____

_____

_____

_____

_____

When you feel like life has knocked the wind out of you and you can
barely put one foot in front of the other, God kneels down to lift you up.
He carries you when you're too weary to keep forging ahead. He nourishes
your heart with soul food and eases your mind with the sweet water of peace.

God is our Father, and He loves us and knows what is best. His will is the very most blessed thing that can come to us under any circumstance.

HANNAH WHITALL SMITH

How abundant are the good things that you have stored up for those who fear you,
that you bestow in the sight of all, on those who take refuge in you.

I love the LORD because he hears my voice and my prayer for mercy. Because he bends down to listen, I will pray as long as I have breath!

PSALM 116:1-2 NLT

_____

_____

_____

_____

_____

_____

_____

_____

_____

_____

_____

_____

_____

_____

When you come into the presence of God, He draws near to you
to listen to what is on your heart, Delighting in your presence,
He hushes the heavenly host to hear the petitions you bring.
And pleased with every indication of your increasing trust, He receives
your praise and gratitude, responding in Spirit with peace and joy.

We may ask, "Why does God bring thunderclouds and disasters
when we want green pastures and still waters?" Bit by bit,
we find behind the clouds, the Father's feet; behind the lightning,
an abiding day that has no night; behind the thunder, a still
small voice that comforts with a comfort that is unspeakable.

OSWALD CHAMBERS

Now may our Lord Jesus Christ Himself, and our God and Father, who has loved us and given us everlasting consolation and good hope by grace, comfort your hearts.

2 THESSALONIANS 2:16–17 NKJV

Be content with what you have, because God has said,
"Never will I leave you; never will I forsake you."

HEBREWS 13:5 NIV

He wants you to sense His presence. He wants you to trust that when
you are afraid, you can turn to Him and find His peace. When you
are weary, you will find His strength.... And when you are in the
middle of a raging storm, you will find His shelter and provision.

Stormie Omartian

God is like a safe house. He gives peace in the midst of drama. He gives you space to think and regroup. Like a house in a storm, a roof over your head and walls around you won't stop the rain or halt the thunder, but it sure keeps you dry in the midst of it. Open the door and come on in.

*The LORD is my rock, my fortress, and my savior; my God is my rock, in whom
I find protection. He is my shield, the power that saves me, and my place of safety.*

PSALM 18:2 NLT

Don't fret or worry. Instead of worrying, pray. Let petitions and praises shape your worries into prayers, letting God know your concerns.

PHILIPPIANS 4:6 MSG

_____

_____

_____

_____

_____

_____

_____

_____

_____

_____

_____

_____

_____

_____

_____

_____

*He comforts us in all our troubles so that we can comfort others. When they are
troubled, we will be able to give them the same comfort God has given us.*

2 CORINTHIANS 1:4 NLT

Ellie Claire™ Gift & Paper Corp.
Minneapolis, MN 55378
www.ellieclaire.com

It Is Well with My Soul
© 2012 by Ellie Claire™ Gift & Paper Corp.

ISBN 978-1-60936-543-1

Stock or custom editions of Ellie Claire titles may be purchased in bulk for educational,
business, ministry, fundraising, or sales promotional use. For information,
please e-mail specialmarkets@summersidepress.com.

Compiled by Barbara Farmer
Cover and interior design by David Carlson | Gearbox

Printed in China